PEOPLES *of* NORTH AMERICA

Comanche

VALERIE BODDEN

CREATIVE EDUCATION • CREATIVE PAPERBACKS

Published by Creative Education and Creative Paperbacks
P.O. Box 227, Mankato, Minnesota 56002
Creative Education and Creative Paperbacks
are imprints of The Creative Company
www.thecreativecompany.us

Design and production by Christine Vanderbeek
Art direction by Rita Marshall
Printed in China

Photographs by Alamy (Pat Bonish, Bygone Collection, Paul Fearn, IllustratedHistory,
INTERFOTO, PJF Military Collection, Prisma by Dukas Presseagentur GmbH, Vintage Images),
Creative Commons Wikimedia (George Catlin/Smithsonian American Art Museum, Reynolds's
Political Map of the United States/Library of Congress), Dreamstime (Taiga), Getty Images
(Authenticated News, Charles Carpenter/Field Museum Library, Library of Congress, Photo
Josse/Leemage, Science & Society Picture Library), iStockphoto (clintspencer, epantha,
Manook, najin), National Geographic Creative (JOEL SARTORE), Shutterstock (Zack Frank,
SMIRNOVA IRINA, Kokoulina, Marzolino, OHishiapply, Stocksnapper, Tim Roberts
Photography, Transia Design), Smithsonian Institution (Department of Anthropology,
Smithsonian Institution/National Museum of the American Indian), SuperStock (Album/
Oronoz, Christie's Images Ltd., Universal Images Group)

Library of Congress Cataloging-in-Publication Data
Names: Bodden, Valerie, author.
Title: Comanche / Valerie Bodden.
Series: Peoples of North America.
Includes bibliographical references and index.
Summary: A history of the people and events that influenced the North American Indian
tribe known as the Comanche, including chief Quanah Parker and conflicts such as the
Council House Massacre.
Identifiers: LCCN 2017027672 / ISBN 978-1-60818-964-9 (hardcover) /
ISBN 978-1-62832-591-1 (pbk) / ISBN 978-1-64000-065-0 (eBook)
Subjects: LCSH: Comanche Indians—History—Juvenile literature.
Classification: LCC E99.C85 B64 2018 / DDC 978.004/974572—dc23

CCSS: RI.5.1, 2, 3, 5, 6, 8, 9; RH.6-8.4, 5, 6, 7, 8, 9

First Edition HC 9 8 7 6 5 4 3 2 1
First Edition PBK 9 8 7 6 5 4 3 2 1

PEOPLES of NORTH AMERICA

Comanche

VALERIE BODDEN

CREATIVE EDUCATION • CREATIVE PAPERBACKS

Table of Contents

A COMANCHE GIRL (ON PAGE 3); A MODERN
CELEBRATION INCLUDING A COMANCHE DANCE IN
NEW MEXICO (PICTURED HERE).

North America's southern Great Plains region was once known as *Comanchería*—the Spanish name for the homeland of the Comanche Indians. Covered with sweet-smelling low grasses, this vast land stretched for hundreds of miles, broken only by the occasional stands of cottonwood trees that lined the region's shallow rivers. In some places, steep buttes rose up from the grasslands. Elsewhere, deep canyons cut jagged lines into the earth, providing protection from harsh winter blizzards. In the summer, the sun scorched the land. Streams slowed to a trickle, and dry grasses crunched underfoot. Although the land looked barren, it was anything but. Huge herds of pronghorn and bison (commonly called buffalo in the past) grazed on the abundant grasses. Prairie dogs, armadillos, and jackrabbits scurried through the brush, while the shrieks of eagles, hawks, and vultures filled the air.

The Comanche called themselves *Nermernuh* (also sometimes spelled Numunu), meaning "Our People." The name "Comanche" is likely taken from a Ute Indian word meaning "anyone who wants to fight me all the time." Constantly moving and adapting, the Comanche pushed other native peoples out of the American Southwest. On the southern plains, they set up an unprecedented empire. When their way of life was threatened by Spanish and American newcomers, the Comanche put up a fierce fight. Although they were eventually forced to give up the majority of their land, the Comanche fought hard to hold on to their traditions—a fight that continues today.

COMANCHERÍA GRASSLANDS STRETCHED
NORTH TO COLORADO'S GREAT SAND DUNES.

COMANCHE
Lords of the Plains
PEOPLES of NORTH AMERICA

The Comanche belong to a large group of American Indians speaking languages of the Uto-Aztecan language family. Peoples speaking these related languages once lived throughout western North America and Central America. The Comanche began as a small group, or band, of the Shoshone. This American Indian tribe lived in the Rocky Mountains and western plains of present-day Wyoming and Montana. There they took shelter in bark lodges among the forests. They hunted deer, rabbits, and bighorn sheep. The Shoshone also gathered berries, roots, and seeds. In the winter, they sometimes ventured onto the plains, where they hunted the plentiful bison.

Eventually, many Shoshone moved out of their mountain homes and onto the Great Plains. Most migrated to the northern plains. But in the late 1600s, one group went south. This group came to be known as the Comanche. **ANTHROPOLOGISTS** are unsure what caused the Comanche to split from the main Shoshone tribe. Some believe the expansion of other American Indian groups into Shoshone territory played a role. Others think the Comanche moved south to be near the large bison herds that grazed on the southern plains. Moving south also brought the Comanche closer to the source of an

MILLIONS OF BISON ONCE ROAMED THE GRASS-LANDS OF NORTH AMERICA BUT BECAME NEARLY EXTINCT BY THE EARLY 1900S, THANKS LARGELY TO OVERHUNTING BY SETTLERS.

COMANCHE TRADERS MADE IT POSSIBLE FOR OTHER PLAINS INDIAN TRIBES TO OBTAIN HORSES.

animal that was rapidly changing the Plains Indians' lifestyle—the horse.

Spanish explorers and settlers brought the first horses to North America in the early 1500s. By the late 1600s, horses had completely changed the Comanche way of life. Before horses, people traveled on foot, carrying their supplies on their backs or on a **TRAVOIS** strapped to dogs. Horses allowed the Comanche to range farther, travel faster, and carry more. Bison hunting and warfare became easier as well. One of the first tribes to use horses, the Comanche soon became master horse handlers. They were the first Indians to fully adopt a mounted, **NOMADIC** lifestyle.

The Comanche did not move onto the plains all at once. Instead, small groups of families likely trickled one after another onto the grasslands. In the early and mid-1700s, these Comanche groups began to migrate farther south. They eventually reached parts of Colorado, Kansas, New Mexico, Texas, and Oklahoma. As the Comanche pushed out the Apache and other native peoples, Comanchería expanded. It soon covered 250,000 square miles (647,497 sq km). Comanche groups continued to move into the area, and with abundant bison to feed the people, the population of Comanchería exploded. From about 1,500 people in 1726, the population likely reached 10,000 to 15,000 by 1750. As the Comanche raided and traded for horses, their herds grew as well, totaling nearly 100,000 animals by the late 1700s.

With so many horses, the Comanche couldn't all camp together, or they would quickly exhaust grazing lands. Instead, they broke up into smaller bands for most of the year. The Spanish called these bands *rancherías*. Each ranchería was made up of

⇥⊶≡⊶ HORSE WEALTH ⊶≡⊶⇤

Among the Comanche, horses were considered private property. A man's wealth was measured by the number of horses he owned. A single Comanche warrior might have 250 horses. The wealthiest warriors had herds numbering in the thousands. A man kept his best horses tied up outside his tepee. The others grazed with the rest of the herd at the edges of the camp. In addition to raiding for horses, the Comanche also captured wild horses and bred their own mounts.

related families who traveled and hunted together. Rancherías
might consist of 30 to upwards of 250 people. Generally, rancherías
were named after their headmen. Among the most important
bands were the Yamparika, Kotsoteka, Penateka, and Kwahada.

As the bands traveled the plains, they made their homes in
tepees, which were perfectly suited to their nomadic lifestyle.
These cone-shaped homes were framed by 22 long, wooden poles.
Bison hides that had been sewn together covered the poles. The
hides were sometimes painted with designs or figures. A flap at the
top of the tepee drew out smoke from the fire inside. It could be
closed in bad weather. Inside, the tepee was 12 to 15 feet (3.7–4.6
m) across. Additional bison hides hung from the wall to keep
moisture out and to insulate the tepee in winter. In the summer,
the skins could be rolled up to allow cooling prairie breezes to cir-
culate. Working together, Comanche women could set up a tepee
in 15 minutes; they could have it down in 5.

Once the Comanche moved to the plains, bison made up the
majority of their diet. The liver, brains, and bone marrow were
considered special delicacies and were eaten immediately after the
kill. Other meat was roasted over fires or boiled. Some meat was

⇒══ WAR TACTICS ══⇐ *Comanche warriors could easily shift between small-scale raids using* GUERRILLA *tactics and large-scale military actions involving direct attacks. When massed in large groups, Comanche warriors kept their horses moving to avoid presenting an easy target. Rather than forming battle lines, they encircled the enemy. At times they pretended to retreat or played dead to draw their enemy into an ambush. Comanche tactics led Colonel Richard Irving Dodge to call them the "most mischievously artful of all the United States' Indians."*

dried and stored for the winter. It could also be mixed with berries and nuts to make high-energy pemmican for warriors on the war trail. In addition to bison, the Comanche hunted elk, deer, bears, and pronghorn. If there was a shortage of game, they ate their horses. They gathered wild plants such as grapes, currants, plums, juniper berries, acorns, wild onions, and radishes as well.

Although Comanchería occupied much of the Southwest, the Comanche were not alone on the southern plains. Other tribes such as the Apache, Kiowa, Ute, and Pawnee lived on the fringes of Comanchería. Known as some of the fiercest American Indian warriors, the Comanche fought most of the other Plains tribes at one point or another during their history. For nearly 50 years, they attacked the Apache, eventually pushing them south across the Rio Grande. The Comanche also fought the Pawnee to the north and the Osage to the east. After an initial alliance with the Ute fell apart, the two tribes became enemies. And although the Comanche were at first enemies of the Kiowa, they formed an alliance with that people in 1790.

The southern plains weren't home only to American Indian peoples, however. Spanish settlers lived in parts of present-day

Texas and New Mexico, which were controlled by Spain when the Comanche first arrived in the area. The Comanche conducted frequent raids of the Spaniards' settlements to steal horses as well as women and children, who could be sold as slaves.

Despite their fearsome reputation, the Comanche also established a flourishing trade network. At times they even called truces for the sake of trade before resuming warfare. Horses quickly became their most important trade good. They traded the animals, along with bison meat and robes, in exchange for agricultural produce such as corn, pumpkins, and tobacco and for European goods such as knives, blankets, and guns. In addition to goods, the Comanche traded slaves they had captured in raids on Spanish settlements and other Indian tribes. They sold some of the slaves to other Indian groups. They brought others to Spanish settlements, where the settlers offered ransom payments for their return. Traveling traders from New Mexico, known as *comancheros*, frequently made trips into Comanchería to trade as well.

The combination of trading and raiding soon made the Comanche the most powerful tribe in the Southwest, earning them the designation "lords of the southern plains." The Comanche knew this land was the ideal location for their people. It provided the animals they needed for food, grazing land for their horses, and shelter for their winter camps. No matter what challenges they encountered, they were determined to stay.

Although the Comanche considered themselves one people, they had no formal tribal organization. Instead, Comanche life revolved around the ranchería. Each ranchería made its own decisions about where and when to camp, hunt, and raid. Each ranchería was led by a head chief, or *paraibo*. A paraibo was known for his wealth and generosity, as well as his bravery and skill in battle. Although the paraibo led the band, he did so by **CONSENSUS** rather than by issuing orders. In making decisions, the paraibo was guided by a council made up of all the men in the band. The council discussed issues until they came to a unanimous decision. Anyone who might still disagree with the decision was free to leave that band to join another.

Life within the ranchería changed with the seasons as the people moved to follow the bison and find fresh grazing land for their horses. As the prairie grasses burst into life each spring, the various rancherías spread out through the land. Each ranchería moved frequently to find new pastures for horses that had grown thin during the winter. The men participated in brief hunts to replenish depleted food stores as well.

Summer was the time for raiding and warfare. Sometimes a single ranchería carried out raids on its own. Other times, multiple rancherías

As a mark of his bravery, 19th-century Comanche chief Mow-way wore in his hair the claw of a grizzly bear he had killed.

UNTIL THE 1800S, COMANCHE HEAD-DRESSES WERE MADE OF ERMINE TAILS AND EAGLE FEATHERS.

joined forces for large-scale raids. The night before leaving camp, the warriors held a war dance and prayed to the spirits. Then, with their faces painted and often wearing a headdress of bison horns, the warriors set out. Over the next days or weeks, the warriors marched during the day and camped in the evening, often traveling hundreds of miles. The farthest raids dipped into Mexico, more than 1,000 miles (1,609 km) south of Comanchería.

The Comanche preferred to carry out raids at night, under a full moon. But sometimes they attacked in broad daylight. In addition to taking horses and capturing women and children, they killed any men they encountered.

The Comanche also carried out revenge and territorial wars. These battles could become bloody, with numerous casualties on each side. Skilled horsemen, Comanche warriors rode their mounts into battle, controlling them with voice commands. Young Comanche warriors learned to hang off the side of their horse and shoot arrows under its neck. This way the animal served as a shield.

Sometimes, instead of killing their enemies, the Comanche counted coup (*KOO*). This involved getting close enough to touch the enemy or fight him hand-to-hand. Counting coup was

LIFE AFTER DEATH — *A Comanche who had died was wrapped in a blanket and placed in a cave, ravine, or rocky crevice. Mourners cut their hair and slashed their skin. Then they burned the possessions of the deceased. The Comanche believed that after death, a person's spirit lived on in a land overflowing with game and fast horses. Those who were* SCALPED *could not enter this land, so Comanche warriors defended the bodies of fallen fighters to keep them from suffering this fate.*

considered the greatest act of bravery.

Comanche raiding slowed in the fall as the men turned their attention to the great fall hunt. This hunt would allow the people to store up food for the winter. By this time of the year, the bison were also getting their thick winter coat, which made their hides valuable for trade. Before the hunt, the men prayed to the bison spirit for success. Then the hunting party rode across the plains as a group. When they reached a herd, each hunter acted on his own. Galloping alongside a bison, the hunter stabbed the huge animal with his long lance or shot arrows at it until it went down. Each hunter identified his kill by the arrows in its hide. The hide belonged to the hunter who made the kill. But another man could claim a portion of the meat by counting coup on the bison.

After the fall hunt, the Comanche prepared for winter. Several rancherías settled together along the river valleys of Comanchería. These forested areas offered wood for fires, trees for protection, and grass and cottonwood bark to feed the horses. Comanche winter camps might include thousands of people and stretch for many miles down a riverbank. As the cold weather closed in, the people rarely ventured from their winter camps. Still, life was busy. Many rancherías hosted trade fairs in the winter. The men carried out small-scale bison hunts and raids as well.

While Comanche men focused on hunting and raiding, women took care of the tepee, gathered plants, cooked meals, cared for children, prepared bison hides, and made clothing and other items. According to 19th-century Mexican official José María Sánchez, Comanche women were "real slaves to the men, who occupy themselves with war and hunting only. The wives bring in the animals that are killed, they cut and cure the meat, tan the hides, make the clothes and arms of the men, and care for the horses." A Comanche man often had more than one wife. The first

COMANCHE MEN WORE THEIR HAIR IN TWO LONG BRAIDS THAT WERE SOME-TIMES WRAPPED IN FUR.

wife lived in the main tepee with her husband. The other wives lived in nearby tepees. All the wives worked together to carry out their many domestic duties.

In addition to multiple wives, nearly every Comanche man kept slaves. Most slaves were women and children, since male captives were usually killed. Slaves were expected to carry out the least pleasant tasks. Sometimes, however, the Comanche married female slaves or adopted slave children into their families. In these cases, the slaves were treated as members of the tribe.

Whether born or adopted into the tribe, Comanche children were prized. Babies spent their first 10 months strapped into a **CRADLEBOARD**, where they could watch as their mothers worked around the camp. By the age of four or five, both boys and girls received their first horse and were taught to ride. Because their parents were busy with other duties, Comanche children were often taught by their grandparents. Boys learned to shoot and hunt small game. By the time they were teens, they were expected to care for the horse herd. After a 15- or 16-year-old boy completed his first successful bison hunt, he was ready to go on the war trail. He also completed his first vision quest around that time.

The purpose of a vision quest was to obtain *puha*, or personal power, from a spirit. During his vision quest, a young man climbed to the top of a hill, where he fasted, or went without eating, and prayed for four days in hopes of receiving a vision from a spirit. The Comanche believed spirits could be found in almost any part of nature, from rocks to animals. Different spirits offered help for different needs. For example, eagles were thought to provide strength, while deer offered agility. Wolves bestowed ferocity. People who shared a puha often formed special dance or military societies.

The Comanche saw religion primarily as an individual matter. According to historian Ernest Wallace, "Every man was his own priest and his own prophet—the individual interpreter of the wills and ways of the spirits." But over time, the Comanche began to celebrate religious ceremonies adopted from other tribes. The Sun Dance, for example, included many songs and dances learned from other Plains tribes. The Beaver Ceremony, learned from the Pawnee, was used for curing illnesses.

CIRCLES PAINTED AROUND A HORSE'S EYES WERE BELIEVED TO IMPROVE THE ANIMAL'S SIGHT IN WAR.

COMANCHE

Violent Encounters

PEOPLES *of* NORTH AMERICA

In the 1520s, before the Comanche had moved onto the southern plains, Spanish explorers marched across present-day Mexico, claiming the land for Spain. By the early 1600s, hundreds of Spanish settlers had established villages in present-day New Mexico. Spanish officials first recorded the presence of the Comanche on the southern plains in 1706. That year, a group of Comanche joined with the Ute to threaten Taos, a small village in present-day New Mexico.

Almost from the time they arrived on the southern plains, the Comanche repeatedly attacked the Spanish settlements. The main motivation for these attacks was to obtain horses and captives. The Spaniards could do little to stop the attacks. With so many horses, the Comanche could easily outrun any pursuing force.

Despite the continual attacks, many Spanish settlements also traded peacefully with the Comanche. In some cases, the Comanche traded horses and slaves stolen from one Spanish-controlled region to Spanish settlers in another. At times, the Spanish attempted to slow Comanche raiding by offering gifts. The Comanche gladly accepted these gifts—and demanded more. When the gifts stopped, raids began again. Periodic peace agreements signed between

PREFERRED COMANCHE WEAPONS INCLUDED
BOWS AND ARROWS AND LONG LANCES—WARRIORS
RARELY USED FIREARMS.

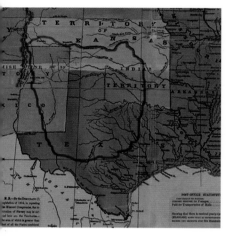

the Spanish and individual Comanche bands rarely lasted, especially since each Comanche band operated separately.

As peace agreements failed and the death toll from raids mounted, the Spanish attempted military action against the Comanche. A military campaign in 1774 resulted in the deaths of 300 Comanche. Another 100 were captured, along with 1,000 horses and mules. The action only angered the Comanche. As Spanish viceroy Antonio María de Bucareli reported, "In place of teaching them lessons, the punishment can have exasperated them and thus be the motivating reason for their uniting to seek the vengeance to which they are accustomed."

The Spanish again mounted a fight in 1779, launching troops into Comanchería. Surprise attacks on Comanche bands continued on and off through 1785, when the Comanche offered to make peace with New Mexico. Although the New Mexican peace lasted, settlers in Texas and Mexico remained vulnerable to Comanche attacks. By the early 1800s, the Comanche were at the height of their power. Their population reached an estimated 20,000 to 40,000, and trading and raiding had made them wealthy.

In 1821, Mexico won its independence from Spain. Mexican settlers flocked onto Comanche lands, and the Comanche stepped up their attacks yet again. The newly independent Mexican government could not afford to buy the Comanche's peace with gifts. But even as raids continued, the Comanche maintained their trade relationship with many Mexican settlements. They sometimes even alternated raiding and trading with the same settlement. On a visit to Mexico, French scientist Jean Louis Berlandier noted how Mexican villagers could tell whether a Comanche visit would prove peaceful: "Whenever they came like this, bringing their

AMERICAN AWE ⟜⟞ *In 1835, George Catlin was among a group of Americans who visited a Comanche village. Catlin was particularly awed by the Comanche welcoming ceremony: "Several hundreds of their braves and warriors came out at full speed to welcome us.... As they wheeled their horses, they very rapidly formed a line ... like a well-disciplined cavalry." Catlin noticed that although his American party was "bristling with arms" and "trespassing in the middle of [Comanche] country," the Comanche carried no weapons on this occasion.*

[wives and children], the visit was a proof of peace, of friendship, and of trust; whereas, when they had only a few women with them, it was because they were at war."

In 1836, Texas broke away from Mexico to form its own republic. The newly independent nation attempted to resolve the Comanche problem by establishing a force of mounted frontiersmen known as the Texas Rangers. Carrying **SIX-SHOOTERS**, the Rangers rode through Texas in pursuit of the Comanche, often engaging them in skirmishes. In 1840, a delegation of Comanche men, women, and children sought peace in San Antonio. In response to earlier Texan demands that they return the hundreds of whites they had taken captive, the Comanche brought with them only one prisoner. Angered, Texas officials took Comanche leaders hostage in the courthouse. The Comanche chiefs refused to promise to return the rest of the captives, saying they couldn't do so because the prisoners were held by other rancherías. When the Comanche tried to escape, soldiers standing guard opened fire at point-blank range. Thirty-five Comanche were killed in what came to be known as the Council House Massacre. Afterward, the Comanche carried out fierce revenge raids.

⟻ **QUANAH PARKER** ⟼ **QUANAH PARKER** *was born around 1852 to a Comanche chief and his white wife, who had been captured by the Comanche as a child. When Quanah was about eight years old, his mother was recaptured by Texas Rangers. A year later, Quanah's father died in battle. At the age of 15, Quanah became chief of the Kwahada band. He led a fierce resistance to settlement on the reservation. After finally surrendering in 1875, he became the first official reservation leader. He died in 1911.*

Meanwhile, growing demand for Comanche horses led the Comanche to expand their raids south of the Rio Grande. By the early 1840s, raiding parties of up to 1,000 warriors struck deep into Mexican territory, killing thousands of Mexicans and stealing hundreds of thousands of horses. Weakened by relentless Comanche raids, Mexico could put up little defense in the **MEXICAN–AMERICAN WAR** that began in 1846. According to historian Brian DeLay, "The Indian raiding certainly influenced the outcome of the U.S.–Mexican War. I think you have to think of the Comanche as important geopolitical players." When the war ended two years later, the southern plains—including Comanchería—passed into the United States' hands. As part of the treaty ending the war, the U.S. government promised to prevent Indian raiders from crossing into Mexico. To keep that promise, American soldiers were quickly dispatched to the southern plains.

At the same time, American settlers flocked to the Southwest. These settlers carried with them diseases such as smallpox and **CHOLERA**. Because the Indians had never been exposed to these diseases, their immune systems were unable to fight them off. An 1849 cholera epidemic killed nearly half the Comanche.

Adding to the devastation, a severe drought struck the southern plains. Grasses died off, and with them so did the bison. The
Comanche turned to eating their horses and mules to avoid starva-
tion, severely reducing their herds. The Comanche trade network
dried up, too, keeping the Comanche from getting needed corn and
other goods. These disasters combined to reduce the Comanche
population from nearly 40,000 to about 10,000 by the mid-1850s.

Meanwhile, the population of Texas exploded, reaching 210,000
by 1850—and people kept coming. They spread across the state,
taking up vast amounts of land for their ranches, cotton planta-
tions, and cornfields. Although they were weakened by disease and
hunger, the Comanche fought back, launching fierce raids across
the state and into Mexico.

In response, the U.S. government established military forts inside the borders of Comanchería. With U.S. soldiers on their land,
Comanche raids slowed by 1853. The next year, the Texas government established a Comanche reservation on the Clear Fork of the
Brazos River in Texas. Suffering from hunger, several hundred
members of the Penateka band settled on the reservation. But this
did not stop other bands from continuing their attacks.

Both the Texas Rangers and the U.S. cavalry responded with
military action. With U.S. forces closing in, the Comanche moved
off the open plains to seek shelter in the canyons of the Texas and
Oklahoma panhandles. Meanwhile, the Penateka Comanche who
had settled on the Clear Fork Reservation were relocated to Indian
Territory (present-day Oklahoma). With the Comanche on the
run, most of Texas opened up for further settlement, and newcomers flooded in. By 1860, the population of Texas had ballooned
to 600,000. The Comanche population, on the other hand, soon
shrank to 5,000.

Just when the Comanche situation looked hopeless, in 1861, troops across Texas withdrew to fight in the American Civil War. The military pressure on them eased, and the Comanche resumed their raids. This drove away many of Comanchería's recent settlers. After the war ended in 1865, few troops were sent back to the area, and Comanche raiding continued largely unchecked. In addition to horses, the Comanche now focused their raids on the millions of cattle grazing on the Texas plains. They also continued to take women and children captive and expected U.S. officials to pay high prices to get them back. As one Indian agent said, "Every prisoner purchased from the Indians amounts to the same as granting them a license to go and commit the same overt act. They boastfully say that stealing white women is more of a lucrative business than stealing horses."

In 1865, the government sought peace with the Comanche through the Treaty of the Little Arkansas. This treaty offered the Comanche a reservation of 40,000 square miles (103,600 sq km) in the heart of Comanchería. In return for the rights to this land, the Comanche promised to allow military forts on their land, to return captives, and to end raids. Chief Drinking Eagle signed the treaty, but he warned the whites that he wouldn't give up any land.

CYNTHIA ANN PARKER (MOTHER OF QUANAH) WAS A COMANCHE CAPTIVE FOR 24 YEARS AND EVENTUALLY MARRIED A WAR CHIEF.

"I am fond of the land I was born on," he said. "The white man has land enough."

Despite Drinking Eagle's proclamation, the Comanche were asked to sign a new treaty in 1867. Known as the Medicine Lodge Creek Treaty, this agreement stated that the government would provide the Comanche with $25,000 a year in goods. In return, the Comanche would relocate to a 5,500-square-mile (14,245 sq km) reservation on traditional Comanche lands in Indian Territory.

Outraged, chief **TEN BEARS** told American officials, "My people have never first drawn a bow or fired a gun against the whites.... It was you who sent out the first soldier.... There are things which you have said to me which I do not like.... You have said that you want to put us on a reservation, to build us houses.... I do not want them. I was born under the prairie, where the wind blew free and there was nothing to break the light of the sun.... I want to die there and not within walls."

Despite such protests, Ten Bears and most of the chiefs eventually signed the treaty to get the promised goods for their people. About a third of the Comanche, most notably members of the Kwahada band, refused and remained on the plains. Even those Comanche who moved onto the reservation didn't stay long. Many settled there in the winter to collect rations. But as soon as the weather warmed, they rode back onto the plains to hunt and raid.

In 1871, the U.S. army launched a full-scale assault on those Comanche still living off the reservation. Companies of cavalry marched across the Texas plains, chasing Comanche bands from one location to another. Their attacks interrupted the Comanche seasonal cycle, making it impossible for the Indians to pasture

Being Comanche

⭐ ══ **CODE TALKERS** ══ ⭐ *During World War II (1939–45), the U.S. military needed a way to send messages the enemy couldn't interpret. They enlisted the help of several American Indians, including 17 Comanche men. These men became known as "code talkers." Using their native language, the code talkers relayed and quickly translated messages. Before this, decoding machines used by the military took several hours to send and decode a message. Code talkers could translate a message in less than three minutes. Their code was never broken.*

their horses, hunt, or prepare for winter. After suffering a devastating attack in September 1872, many Comanche agreed to move onto the reservation.

Still, some Comanche, including the Kwahada band led by Quanah Parker, continued to flee U.S. forces. But the army wasn't the band's only enemy. In the early 1870s, white hunters descended onto the plains. They were after bison hides, which could be sold for high prices back east. The hunters slaughtered the animals by the millions, taking their hides and leaving the meat to rot. The Comanche watched as their most important food source was decimated. Although the white hunters were trespassing on Comanche lands, the government did nothing to stop them. In fact, General **PHILIP HENRY SHERIDAN** encouraged the practice. "Let them kill, skin, and sell until the buffalo is exterminated," he said. "It is the only way to bring lasting peace and allow civilization to advance."

Determined to stop the hunters, Quanah Parker gathered 700 Comanche, Kiowa, Cheyenne, and Arapaho warriors. On June 27, 1874, the warriors launched an attack against 28 hunters at an abandoned trading post known as Adobe Walls. Although greatly outnumbered, the bison hunters were armed with long-range rifles and sheltered by thick walls. Within hours, 15 Indian warriors lay dead, and the rest retreated.

The Battle of Adobe Walls marked the start of the short-lived Red River War (also known as the Buffalo War). By September 1874, an army regiment led by Colonel **RANALD MACKENZIE** had cornered the Comanche at Palo Duro Canyon. Although most of the Comanche there managed to escape, the army burned their tepees and winter supplies and slaughtered their horses. Left with nothing, most Comanche finally moved onto the reservation. The last group to surrender was Quanah Parker's Kwahada band, in June 1875.

THE SECOND-LARGEST CANYON IN THE U.S., PALO DURO CANYON IS NOW A TEXAS STATE PARK.

No longer forced to wear American clothing (right), Comanche celebrate their heritage in traditional dress at festivals (above).

Quanah Parker quickly became the principal chief on the reservation. Although he had held out the longest against settling on the reservation, he now encouraged the Comanche to adapt to their new conditions. But life on the reservation was hard. Officials forced the Comanche to adopt white ways, including American-style homes and clothing. Although they had always been hunters, the Comanche were now expected to become farmers and ranchers. Comanche children were forced to attend boarding schools far from home, where they were punished for speaking their own language. In 1901, the government broke the reservation into **ALLOTMENTS**. Each Comanche was given 160 acres (64.7 ha) of land from the reservation. Any land left over after allotment was opened to white settlement. After years of war, disease, and hunger, the Comanche population dropped to 1,400 by 1904.

Over the years, conditions improved, and the Comanche population bounced back. Today, an estimated 16,000 people

⊸⟹ JOHNNY DEPP, HONORARY COMANCHE ⟸⊷ *For his role as American Indian guide Tonto in the 2013 film* The Lone Ranger, *actor Johnny Depp consulted with several Comanche Indians. Depp, who believes he may have some Indian ancestry, said that the American Indians he worked with on the film "gave me the passion and drive to build my character with great care." After the film's release, Depp was adopted as an honorary member of the Comanche tribe. In recognition of his acting abilities, he was given the name Mah-Woo-Meh, meaning "shape-shifter."*

identify as Comanche. About half of the Comanche population lives in Oklahoma on land that generations ago made up part of Comanchería. Many lease their allotted land for cattle ranching or oil drilling.

TODAY, THE COMANCHE, KIOWA, AND OTHER PLAINS TRIBES JOIN TOGETHER FOR TRADITIONAL DANCES AND CELEBRATIONS.

Although their traditional culture was nearly wiped out, many Comanche are focused on reviving it. By 2006, fewer than 150 people still spoke the Comanche language. But more than a decade later, many young people still participate in Comanche language classes at Comanche Nation College in Lawton, Oklahoma. As student Gordon Tahquechi said, "Every time an elder dies, one more of our speakers is gone. I wanted to do something in my lifetime to keep the language alive." Other traditions are kept alive through the annual powwow, where singers and dancers from many tribes gather. The Comanche way of life has changed greatly over the past 400 years. From their early days as a band of the Shoshone to their triumph as "lords of the southern plains" to their clashes with Spanish and American forces, the Comanche have faced many challenges. Through them all, they have adapted while fiercely protecting their traditions and culture.

Like most American Indian peoples, the Comanche placed a high value on their traditional stories. These stories shared customs, taught lessons, or immortalized the actions of Comanche heroes. Many stories explained the origin of the Comanche people and aspects of nature. In this story, a young girl teaches her people about generosity—a characteristic highly valued by the Comanche. The story also explains how the bluebonnet flower came to be.

The Comanche were a prosperous people, spread out all across the southern plains. Every spring, the spirits sent rain to water the earth and bring grasses to feed the bison. But one spring, a terrible drought fell. All the bison died or wandered away, and the people began to starve. Then a terrible sickness struck the people. Many died.

The people believed these things were happening because they had angered the spirits. They held a dance to learn what the spirits wanted. The spirits told the people that they had become too selfish. They said the people took from the land but never gave anything back. In order to make up for this, the spirits said the people must sacrifice the most important possession in the whole tribe. After they burned the item, they needed to spread its ashes to the four winds.

The people discussed the spirits' request. One man said he was sure the spirits didn't mean his horse when they asked for the people's most valuable possession. A woman said it couldn't be her bison robe. Yet another person was certain the spirits didn't want his bow.

As the people continued to talk, a little girl named She-Who-Is-Alone looked at her toy doll. The doll was made of cornhusks. Its eyes and mouth were painted on with berry juice. In its hair was a bright blue feather from a blue jay. The doll was the girl's most valuable possession. Her parents, who had both died of sickness, had given it to her.

She-Who-Is-Alone knew what she had to do. She climbed to the top of a hill and lit a fire. Then, with one last look at her doll, she tossed it into the flames. After the doll had burned up, She-Who-Is-Alone scooped up its ashes. She spread them to the north, south, east, and west. Too sad to return to her village, she slept on the hilltop.

When She-Who-Is-Alone woke up the next morning, the hills all around her were covered with beautiful flowers. The flowers were the same color as the feather in the doll's hair. Amazed, all the people joined the girl on the hill. As they thanked the spirits, rain began to fall. The drought ended, and the bison returned to the plains. Ever since that time, the spirits have sent the blue flowers—called bluebonnets—every spring to honor the girl, who was given a new name—She-Who-Dearly-Loved-Her-People.

ALLOTMENTS
portions set aside for individuals; many American Indians were forced to take allotments from tribal lands, with any remaining lands going to the U.S. government

ANTHROPOLOGISTS
people who study the physical traits, cultures, and relationships of different peoples

CHOLERA
a disease that causes nausea, vomiting, diarrhea, and severe dehydration

CONSENSUS
agreement by all or most of a group

CRADLEBOARD
a board or frame to which an infant could be strapped to be carried on the back

GUERRILLA
having to do with fighting tactics that involve undercover movements and surprise attacks, usually carried out by a small, independent group of fighters

INDIAN AGENT
someone assigned to deal with specific Indian tribes on the government's behalf

MEXICAN–AMERICAN WAR
fought from 1846 to 1848 between the U.S. and Mexico over the territory of Texas, the conflict resulted in the U.S. gaining control over the lands of the American Southwest

NOMADIC
moving from place to place rather than living in a permanent home

PHILIP HENRY SHERIDAN
(1831–88) U.S. cavalry officer who helped lead federal forces to victory in the Civil War before serving in Indian wars in the western U.S.

QUANAH PARKER
(c. 1852–1911) son of a Comanche chief and white mother who became chief of the Kwahada band of Comanche and led his people in the fight against U.S. forces attempting to push them onto a reservation; after surrendering in 1875, he became the first official reservation leader

RANALD MACKENZIE
(1840–89) U.S. military officer who fought in the Civil War before being sent to fight the Comanche and Kiowa on the southern plains

SCALPED
to have the skin at the top of the head, with the attached hair, cut off as a battle trophy

SIX-SHOOTERS
guns that can hold six bullets at one time

TEN BEARS
(c. 1792–1872) chief of the Yamparika band of Comanche who was known for his eloquent speeches and favored peace with the whites, even though he resented their presence on tribal lands; on two occasions, he traveled to Washington, D.C., to unsuccessfully seek concessions for his people

TRAVOIS
a vehicle made of two poles crossed into a V-shape at one end, with a bison hide hung between them to serve as a platform; the travois was hitched to a dog or horse, with the ends dragging on the ground

Brown, Dee. *Bury My Heart at Wounded Knee: An Indian History of the American West.* New York: Sterling, 2009.

Fehrenbach, T. R. *Comanches: The History of a People.* New York: Anchor Books, 2003.

Hämäläinen, Pekka. *The Comanche Empire.* New Haven, Conn.: Yale University Press, 2008.

Kavanagh, Thomas W. "Comanche" in *Plains,* ed. Raymond J. DeMallie. Vol. 13, bk. 2 of *Handbook of North American Indians.* Ed. William C. Sturtevant. Washington, D.C.: Smithsonian, 2001.

Malinowski, Sharon, Anna Sheets, and Linda Schmittroth, eds. *Arctic & Subarctic, Great Plains, Plateau.* Vol. 3 of *UXL Encyclopedia of Native American Tribes.* Detroit, Mich.: UXL, 1999.

Neeley, Bill. *The Last Comanche Chief: The Life and Times of Quanah Parker.* New York: Wiley, 1995.

Powell, Eric. "Searching for the Comanche Empire." *Archaeology,* May/June 2014. Ebsco: MasterFile Premier.

Wishart, David, ed. *Encyclopedia of the Great Plains Indians.* Lincoln: University of Nebraska Press, 2007.

↞⊨ READ MORE ⊨↠

Collinson, Clare, ed. *Peoples of the East, Southeast, and Plains.* Redding, Conn.: Brown Bear Books, 2009.

Streissguth, Thomas. *The Comanche.* San Diego: Lucent Books, 2000.

↞⊨ WEBSITES ⊨↠

COMANCHE NATIONAL MUSEUM AND CULTURAL CENTER
http://www.comanchemuseum.com/
Take a virtual tour of the Comanche Museum to learn more about the Comanche culture and way of life.

NATIONAL MUSEUM OF THE AMERICAN INDIAN: NATIVE WORDS, NATIVE WARRIORS
http://nmai.si.edu/education/codetalkers/
Learn more about the code talkers and how they helped the U.S. military during World War II.